WILD HORSES
OF AMERICA

Text and Captions by L. Edward Purcell

Commissioning Editor
Trevor Hall

Designer
Philip Clucas MSIAD

Photography
Claude Poulet

Production Director
Gerald Hughes

Editorial Director
David Gibbon

Publishing Director
Ted Smart

CLB 1823
Copyright © 1987 Colour Library Books Ltd.,
  Guildford, Surrey, England.
Printed and bound in Barcelona, Spain by Cronion, S.A.

Published 1987 by Portland House
Distributed by Crown Publishers, Inc.
ISBN 0 517 63116 4
h g f e d c b a

WILD HORSES
OF AMERICA

Text by
L. EDWARD PURCELL

PORTLAND HOUSE

You hear and feel them first – their drumbeat of flight vibrating the earth.

A band of mustangs bursts from a narrow ravine. Led by an older mare, their heads are high, their shaggy manes flow in the rush, and their long, unkempt tails stream behind like proud banners.

The stallion runs easily at the rear of the band, herding his mares with nips and signals, but alert all the while for any hint of danger.

He's not so big as imagined and his coat has never felt a groom's brush, yet the sight of him quickens your blood and lights visions in the mind.

A free-roaming band reminds us vividly that horses evolved in nature as fleet and powerful plains animals, finely coordinated bundles of nerve connected to masses of muscle and bone. Horses are machines designed to eat and run. No matter how long we humans have regarded horses as a source of power or speed for our own purposes, the wild horse reasserts the truth that equines are domestic in only the most fragile sense.

Yet there is something about wild horses that swells the human spirit. We see freedom incarnate and we want to be part of it, if only in our imaginations. We see a workaday slug, once consigned to pulling wagons, plowing fields, and transporting riders, now roaming at will across vast tracts of beautiful landscape, required only to feed itself, mate, and go where the winds of chance and instinct blow.

As J. Frank Dobie wrote: "No one who conceives him as only a potential servant to man can apprehend the mustang. The true conceiver must be a true lover of freedom – a person who yearns to extend freedom to all life."

A wild horse doesn't need humans, it needs only to be left alone.

Tens of thousands of wild horses live today in the American West, protected from their only remaining important predator – man. Once the herds numbered in the millions, before settlement pushed them off the Great Plains and mustangers hunted them down for pet food. As recently as the late 1960s, the end seemed near, but now herds of wild horses thrive to the point they wander into Nevada housing developments to nibble the flowers beds. Others hide in mountain enclaves, protected as much by rugged terrain as by man-made law.

The story of the wild horse in America includes Spanish-helmeted Conquistadores, buffalo-hunting Indians, hard-riding cowboys, and grade-school children scribbling urgent letters to Congressmen.

Wild horses are an indelible part of the American West – living symbols of romance, adventure, and freedom.

America's wild horses aren't really wild, at least not in the way lions and tigers and bears are wild.

Technically, wild horses are "feral" – formerly domesticated animals that have gained freedom and now live apart from humans. The distinction is not terribly important, since horses re-acquire their ancient wild instincts and abilities very rapidly when separated from human care.

All the horses that now roam freely in the Americas are either offspring of animals introduced from Europe by the Spanish over four centuries ago or descendants of more recent imports from Northern Europe via the Eastern United States.

When the Spanish invaders under Hernando Cortez brought 13 horses ashore onto a Mexican beach in 1519, there were no other such animals anywhere in all the vast reaches of North and South America. The native peoples had never seen a horse, and they understandably found the beasts to be terrifying curiosities, especially when ridden by armor-clad Conquistadores.

The only true wild species of horse left in the world today may be a Mongolian breed, Przewalski's Horse, but there is considerable doubt that even that obscure line still lives wild somewhere on an Asian plain. All other horse breeds are now domestic, although closely related to several species of wild zebras and wild asses.

Yet the horse originated in North America so far as the fossil records show. The tale of the horse's ancient development and travel is as circuitous as it is interesting.

The first known evidences of a horse-like creature are fossil remains of the Eohippus ("dawn horse"), a tiny, rat-like animal scarcely a foot tall at the shoulder, with three toes, little resembling the modern horse. Eohippus lived 50 or 60 million years ago, both in North America and Europe (including the British Isles, where the first fossils were discovered). Earth scientists presume the two land masses were then linked, and before the continents broke apart and drifted an ocean's length, the dawn horse left fossils in both places. The Eohippus line seems to have reached a dead end in Europe, but continued to develop in North America.

Over the majestic and incomprehensible time span of evolution, primitive horses grew in stature, lost toes, changed teeth, and, eventually, disappeared from North America for tens of thousands of years. They survived, however, where they had crossed over into Asia and developed into the modern horse, Equus caballus. As far as scientists can interpret, horses returned to the American continent about 600,000 years ago, presumably re-crossing a land bridge at the Bering Straits.

Then, about 12,000 years ago, the horse again became extinct in America, this time for good; part of a wave of extinctions that continue to baffle paleontologists. For whatever reasons – meteor impacts, overhunting by early humans, change of climate – horses ceased to exist where they had once (really twice) been abundant.

However, their Asian and European cousins lived on. Within another few thousand years, wild horses had spread from the plains of Asia to the forests of Europe and humans ceased merely to hunt horses for food and began to capture and manage the animals for specific purposes: warfare, agriculture and transportation. Horsetamers brought their charges into the Middle East by 2,000 B.C. and developed special breeds suited to the hot, dry climate. The eventual results were animals of moderate stature but considerable speed and endurance, and often of surpassing beauty.

To the north, in the colder climes of the European forestlands, other types of horses, larger, slower, but on the whole more powerful, evolved through selective breeding.

The two types met in Spain, where the Islamic invaders from North Africa brought with them a hardy Barb horse (called so after the Berbers) bred for the desert. In Andalusia, a new strain emerged, mixing the Barb traits with a dash of northern cold blood to produce a distinctive and at the time famous and much-sought horse, the Spanish jennet.

Twenty of these animals sailed with Christopher Columbus on his second voyage to the New World in 1494. Their trip must have been incredible, since they were slung up by the bellies for the entire journey, receiving scant water and feed. Nonetheless, most of them arrived in reasonable health, and the Spanish began breeding stations on the islands of Hispaniola and Cuba.

The caballeros of Cortez and the other Spanish military expeditions probably didn't realize there were no native horses when they first stepped on the mainland, but it didn't take the invaders long to grasp that the Indian peoples had never before seen such animals. The military advantages were obvious and the Conquistadores played them to full value.

Within a few decades, Spain controlled Mexico, Central America, and considerable parts of South America. More and more horses were imported from Europe and bred in the Caribbean islands, so by the time of Francisco Coronado's grand expedition northward across the Rio Grande in 1539, he could include 200 horses in his force. While the lure of gold and silver moved most of the Spaniards to adventure in the New World, others saw the promise of the land, and large cattle ranches were established in northern Mexico by the end of the 16th century, advancing in concert with the missionizing priests.

In 1598, Juan Oñate settled large numbers of soldiers, missionaries and ranchers in modern-day New Mexico. Horses were vital to herding cattle and no self-respecting Spaniard of a certain class would walk when he could ride, so more and more horses were shipped in or foaled.

The Spanish masters long resisted training the converted Indians to horsemanship, suspecting correctly that to allow Indians access to horses was to shift power towards what were essentially enslaved people. But the need for mounted herders was too great, so in 1621 the edict against supplying horses to Indians was removed.

Thus began the great herds of wild horses in America and a breathtaking cultural transformation of the native tribes of the deserts and plains, for Indian vaqueros soon learned that to own a horse was the next thing to freedom.

Horses flowed away from the Spanish ranches and onto the plains. Some strayed, some were stolen. Whatever their origin, within a short time bands of wild horses discovered a new world which seemed perfectly made for them.

Similar in many ways to the North African deserts where the breed began, and to the Asian steppes of even more ancient species history, the great Southwest and Central Plains of America provided an ideal environment for wild horses. There were vast, open spaces, millions and millions of square miles virtually uninhabited. There was ample water in most places and abundant graze. There were few predators dangerous enough to thin the growing horse population. Horses shared the range with other large grazers and browsers (horses can be either if need be) in the form of great herds of American buffalo and antelope, but the West was big enough to support them all.

Nature and instinct took hold as the horse herds grew and grew for the next 150 years. Separated by the natural barrier of the Rockies, two rivers of horseflesh moved northward, one through Texas up onto the plains, reaching Canada by mid-18th century, the other along the eastern edge of the Great Basin, northward to present-day Idaho and then to Oregon, branching to fill the valleys of California along the way.

As for the native people of North America, seldom in the history of humankind has there been an example of greater impact on a culture than that of the horse on the Indian. Previously sedentary or semi-nomadic people were transformed into mobile, prosperous tribes by acquisition of the horse. The Concho, the Caddo, the Kiowa, the Navajo, the Pueblo, the Shoshone, the Ute, the Sioux, the Mandan, the Crow, the Cayuse, the Yakima, the Nez Percé, the Blood, and many, many more Indian peoples in succession discovered the horse, as trading spread the miraculous animal from tribe to tribe.

No longer were the plains people tied to circumscribed hunting grounds or consigned to nip inefficiently at the buffalo on foot. Bands could move at will, follow the herds, seek better places. Warfare became fluid, a matter of far-reaching and quick strikes against an enemy – and how better to hurt than to steal a rival's horse?

For many tribes the horse came to be the center of economic, social, and cultural life. Wealth and status were measured by the quantity and quality of horses owned. The tough, little Spanish horse was perfectly suited for the rough grazing and rigorous life of an Indian pony, whether pulling a laden travois, riding resolutely to war, or plunging sure-footed alongside a racing buffalo bull.

If the supply of horseflesh ran thin, it was always possible to capture new animals from the ever-growing wild herds. Most tribes used relays of riders to run wild horses to exhaustion and then rope them. Occasionally, it was possible to capture larger numbers at one time within a "great circle" of riders. Both of these methods were invented early and not much improved on by any horse hunters until the 20th century.

Some tribes, such as the Comanche, who were renowned as the most skilled riders ever to straddle a horse, gained their mounts through trade. Others developed careful breeding practices, which in the case of the Nez Percés resulted in the glorious Appaloosa strain. The Cayuse tribe, since virtually disappeared, once owned so many horses that their name was adopted to mean any Indian pony.

There was probably an easy interchange between Indian herds and wild horse bands, and the population of free-roaming horses was doubtlessly fed by large numbers of horses that strayed from the Spanish ranches and settlements. Some romantic souls have tried out the theory that the huge wild horse herds that eventually covered the plains and deserts of the West originated from the first liberated horses of Coronado or Hernando DeSoto, but that is extremely unlikely. The evidence is strong that most of the wild horses came from Spanish ranches and towns, passing off and on through Indian hands perhaps, but mostly growing by escape and natural increase.

"Mustang," the most familiar name for wild horses, springs from a corruption of the term "mesteno," referring to a type of Spanish stock-raiser's association that claimed strays. As the Spanish attempted to settle the southern fringes of the Great Plains, they discovered keeping horses on the edge of open rangeland was difficult, and strays became the rule rather than the exception.

By the late 18th century, travelers in Texas reported breathtaking numbers of wild horses north of the Rio Grande. Fray Morfi, a Franciscan diarist, wrote in 1777 of seeing herds "so abundant that their trails make the country utterly uninhabited by people look as if it were the most populated in the world. All the grass on the vast ranges has been consumed by them, especially around the waterings."

The first ranchers in Texas were simply overwhelmed by the wild horses. It was nearly impossible to hold on to a string of domestic stock in the face of repeated raids by wild stallions searching for a new supply of mares. And, without fences, the task of controlling ranch stock was a nightmare. In 1806, for example, a single herd of 736 horses escaped in mass after being spooked by a party of nearby hunters.

By the middle years of the 19th century, about the time of the Mexican-American War, some sections of Texas were completely overrun with wild horse herds. One of the most famous observations of this sea of animals was by the young American Army lieutenant, Ulysses S. Grant, whose experience still stirred his memories nearly 40 years later:

"The column halted for a rest, and a number of officers, myself among them, rode out two or three miles to see the extent of the herd. The country was a rolling prairie, and, from the higher ground, the vision was obstructed only by the earth's curvature. As far as the eye could reach to our right, the herd extended. To the left, it extended equally. There was no estimating the animals in it; I have no idea that they could all have been coralled in the State of Rhode Island, or Delaware, at one time. If they had been, they would have been so thick that the pasturage would have given out the first day."

Historian Frank J. Dobie estimated that the high point of the Texas herds came around 1848. He believed there may have been as many as 2 million wild horses on the Texas plains alone, and there is no evidence to contradict his numbers.

Farther west, on the Pacific side of the Rockies, conditions were not quite so favorable for the proliferation of wild horse herds, but American travelers to California encounterd impressive herds in the fertile valleys and on the edges of the desert. Herds were reported as far north as the Columbia River basin – the home of the Cayuse tribe – and a traveler in 1816 recounted individual herds of more than 700.

There is no way to know for certain, or even within a reasonable distance of certainty, how many wild horses roamed the West at the climax of the population, but even sober guessers put the total at between three and five million.

Not all wild horses lived west of the Mississippi, however. Smaller bands lived in the Eastern United States, mostly in the more remote areas, removed from agriculture. There are several reports dating from the late 17th century of wild horse bands in the Blue Ridge region of Virginia. They, too, most likely sprang from strays, but in addition to Spanish stock from Florida there was probably a mixture of cold-blooded lines from heavy horses brought to New Amsterdam by the Dutch, and lighter horses imported by the British settlers.

The most famous wild horses of the East are the ponies of Assateague Island, off the coast of Virginia. Very small in stature (probably due to generations of sparse pasturage) these wild horse survivors are rounded up each year and swum to the mainland where the culls are sold to help support a local volunteer fire department. Their lives were immortalized by Marguerite Henry's famous account of "Misty of Chincoteague" in a much-loved and best-selling children's book. The Assateague ponies are most likely the remnants of horses that swam to the island from the mainland, but some believe they may have originated from animals escaping a Spanish shipwreck.

The heyday of the wild horse in the West, however, was over when the first American cattle rancher moved out onto the Great Plains. Organized agriculture, even the loosely organized style of the western cattle grazer, and wild horses do not mix. In addition, the Homestead Act unleashed a wave of sodbusters westward after the Civil War. Within a few decades, the once unpopulated reaches of wild horse country had become home to cattle and crops, often fenced with barbed wire. The buffalo were nearly exterminated, and the horizon-stretching horse herds were reduced to living in those places humans didn't often venture.

And, as humans came to live in closer proximity to wild horses, they began to intrude on the genetic strain of the pure Spanish mustang. Stray horses from ranches mixed many kinds of breeding into the wild horse bands, and often ranchers intentionally turned out large stallions, such as Percherons, to "breed up" nearby herds which they then hoped to capture and sell.

By the end of the 19th century there were still hundreds of thousands of wild horses in the American West, but nothing like the millions of only 50 years before. Moreover, the largest concentrations were in pockets removed from the prime grazing lands of the central plains. More and more, horse bands sought the foothills and the desert edges west of the Rockies.

Horses prefer to live in small family bands. Even the great horizon-to-horizon herds of the 19th century were probably made up of many smaller bands, and today's wild horses seldom form groups with more than a dozen members – frequently as few as four or five. Almost never does a wild horse choose to live alone.

Horses also keep a strict social order, with a single dominant stallion at the top. Much of the time the band is led in daily activities by a senior mare, followed by other mares in an established sequence. Foals and young horses under reproductive age fall into the band hierarchy on their own or as attachments to their mothers when physically close to the mare.

This is essentially a harem arrangement. The stallion is the primary animal in each band, and the mares he attracts or captures stay with the group at least in part because of the stallion's physical coercion. The younger animals remain with the family harem only so long as they are not sexually active – when colts and fillies reach the age of two or three, they are forced out of the band to form new attachments.

Thus, family bands are the basic units of the wild horse world.

The stallion's role is to breed, keep the band together, and defend the group against outside threats, such as rival males or predators. For the most part this makes for a life of constant vigilance, broken by periods of intense activity – either headlong flight or confrontation with other stallions. The head stallion of a wild horse band tends to be extremely possessive of his mares, and he controls them closely so long as there is any hint of outside interference. Much of the stallion's time is spent at the edge of the band, looking out for danger.

On a day-to-day basis, however, the dominant mare often makes many of the routine decisions about the band's movement and activity, apparently choosing the places to feed and even when to seek water. The greatest responsibility of the senior mare is to lead the band in flight when escaping from danger. She runs at the head of the group, selecting the route. The other mares follow in rank order, with the stallion at the rear in a position to defend the band or nip at stragglers.

Old-time mustang hunters, if they were seeking to capture good riding stock, seldom bothered to chase a stallion that ran at the head of his harem. They realized such an animal was untrustworthy and would likely high-tail it over the next rise rather than protect his mares. The mustangers viewed this as a sign that the horse lacked character.

The social status of the mares determines which drinks first at a watering place (along with her offspring) and which gets the attention of the stallion if more than one mare is in heat at the same time. The males themselves appear to be relatively uninterested in how this social order is maintained, expending most of their energy toward external matters and on breeding. Human observers have been unable to figure out exactly what controls the status of mares – in some cases it seems to be age or size, in other cases there is no discernible pattern.

Mares often show surprising independence from the dominant male of the band, and a few have even been observed living with a foal slightly apart from the basic family unit. A dominant mare is probably most important to a band with a young and inexperienced stallion, perhaps one who has only recently defeated the reigning stud of the group. A young stallion has to rely on an older mare, and she often takes his gestures of dominance with little grace, sometimes kicking or biting back. Whatever the situation, if a band's stallion is preoccupied in dealing with an outside threat, the dominant mare will usually assume the role of watcher and leader.

The position of younger horses in a family band is always a bit tenuous. Foals are tied closely to their mothers and receive little direct attention from the stallion or even from other mares. As the horses grow older, however, the maternal relationship weakens. Fillies are not usually accepted permanently as part of the band – belying an old western belief that stallions regularly practiced incestuous inbreeding – and are driven out when they reach a certain age. Young males suffer the same fate as soon as they show signs of being interested in the mares and thus becoming a threat to the dominance of the stallion.

The result is, of course, that in any given wild horse population there is a surfeit of young, unattached male animals, old enough to desire mates but too green to defeat a dominant stallion. These young bachelors usually form their own bands, based on frustration and the need for company. Full of what appears to be youthful, high-spirited energy, such bachelor bands are fragile and tend to break up and re-form often.

Mock combat is a frequent pastime among all-male bands, as young stallions practice behavior they will eventually need if they are ever to establish their own harems. There is much posturing and playful sparring. Nonetheless, the bachelors often appear to be insecure and not quite certain how to respond to outside threats.

It's tempting to compare juvenile wild horse bands to gangs of teenage boys.

A few family bands contain more than one stallion, but in such cases one of the two is clearly the leader. The stallions divide guard responsibilities, and may even share mares, but there is usually an observable undercurrent of tension between the two males that may surface at any time. Recurring battles and challenges often mark multi-stallion arrangements.

There are very few instances of solitary wild horses. Probably the only cases are older stallions which have been driven out of polite society after losing a harem to a younger stud. Even when this happens, older horses may attempt to join a band of juvenile males rather than wander alone. The social instinct is strong.

Competition among dominant males, however, is the cornerstone of wild horse existence. Life for the stallion is a continuous round of challenge and defense. As one observer of wild horses puts it: "a stallion is always the most active member of a band, for maintaining its integrity is the paramount task in his life." Thus, much of a stallion's behavior is aggressive, directed toward other stallions who want to take what he has: the harem of mares. Most of the aggression stops short of violence, and stallions employ a well-honed repertory of gestures and sounds that display aggressive attitudes but involve little chance for actual injury. When a dominant stallion is challenged, he lays back his ears, snorts, paws, screams, weaves his lowered head back and forth while making bite threats, and generally tries to intimidate his opponent by a fearsome show. In fact, wild horses are conservative when it comes to actual violence, and they tend to use the minimum of force and the maximum of bluster whenever possible. The object is to draw a signal of submission from the challenger without harm.

Occasionally, this just isn't enough, and a real fight between stallions erupts. When this happens, it's an awesome display of speed, strength, and agility by large and powerful animals. Seldom does stallion combat result in death for the vanquished, but serious injury is not uncommon and almost all wild stallions carry scars and marks of battle.

The truly earnest frays begin with few preliminaries, perhaps no aggressive display at all.

The principal weapons are teeth and hooves. The stallions charge and whirl and bump one another, each trying for a telling bite or a stunning kick. They may rear to strike with forelegs or to attempt a neck bite. The sound and the fury and the energy expended are frighteningly impressive to humans who have witnessed them:

"The combatants met each other walking on hind legs, striking with forefeet, ears laid back, mouths open, teeth bared. They raked the hide from each other, made deep cuts. They screamed. Their teeth slipping off firm flesh clicked together. They sought jugular veins. They lunged their whole weight against each other. Now one or both whirled with catlike rapidity and kicked like a pile-driver."

Almost all such violent confrontations result from sexual competition. Band stallions have a monopoly on wild mares, and unless a bachelor can defeat a dominant stud horse, there's not much opportunity for mating and reproduction. Fights between reigning stallions are much less common than combat between a mare-owning stallion and an unattached male.

The fierce competition for females among stallions probably contributes to maintaining the vigor of a specific wild horse population – all other factors being equal – because lesser males have little opportunity to contribute to the gene pool of the herd's offspring.

The innate sociability of wild horses may, in certain situations, overcome the competitive spirit, and several bands may live in relative proximity, forming a larger herd unit in a loose sort of way. Observers have been hard pressed to understand the herd phenomenon completely, but it appears that if food and water are ample and the horses are not threatened by outside predators, bands may share territory much of the time, although the band structure is still evident. Herding may also result from exactly the opposite conditions: if horses are crowded onto inadequate range, social order tends to break down under pressure.

Bands seldom move outside a well-defined home range that encompasses a relatively small area – typically 15 to 20 square miles. Weather and forage conditions may change this pattern, but in the absence of unusual pressures, wild horse bands spend most of their time close to familiar water sources and eating in familiar places. Several bands may share part or all of common home range, taking turns at water holes and rotating between grazing areas. Mustang hunters learned to rely on the band's preference for one range, and discovered quickly that horses returned to familiar places after being chased. There is a difference of scientific opinion about whether wild horses are strongly territorial. Most animals defend a territory from outsiders, although the intensity of this pattern varies from species to species. Since wild horse bands typically share the same general home range, using resources in turn, they don't exhibit much exclusivity, and the aggressive confrontations between stallions are more likely caused by sexual competition than by a desire to defend a specific territory.

A fascinating sidelight to band interaction is the wild-horse habit of building up mounds of dung, called "stud piles." Apparently only the stallions contribute to such mounds, and any passing stud adds his contribution. The piles may reach considerable heights along well-travelled routes in areas of high population density.

Although they prefer grasses, wild horses will eat almost anything that grows in their habitat – which explains why horses are so tenacious of survival and why cattlemen so dislike having very many wild horses on the range.

Horses are primarily grazers, eating a variety of wild grasses. As the horse developed over the millennia, its teeth evolved into remarkable tools for clipping and chewing large quantities of coarse grass. A horse is able to snip off grasses close to the roots and then, disregarding the grit and sand included, grind the tough fibers between very hard enamel tooth ridges. As a horse ages and these enamel ridges wear low, the animal's teeth shift to maintain a constant, level grinding surface. One cause of death in old horses is the final loss of enamel, bringing on starvation.

If grass is scarce, horses can also subsist by browsing on bark, buds, leaves, and other rough eating. Their digestive systems – unlike the cow's – can handle high fiber/low protein diets with relative ease. They can even thrive on aquatic plants, although this is a problem seldom presented to the wild horse, whose major habitat is usually dry.

Wild horses, particularly stallions, keep a constant vigil while grazing. They typically position themselves parallel to the wind direction before dipping their heads to clip a mouthful. The head is brought erect to check the wind and the horizon before chewing.

Much of a wild horse's time is spent eating. Wild herds have been observed to graze for almost 75 percent of their waking hours during winter and spring, moving from patch to patch. In part, the horse needs to feed constantly because of its relatively inefficient digestive system. The same biological mechanism that allows horses successfully to eat rough browse also limits the nutrition it can wring from food.

In winter, when snow covers the grasses, horses paw to uncover food. Unless snow accumulates very deeply or crusts over too much, horses are still able to feed well in the winter and survive harsh weather much more readily than cattle or sheep, both of which become helpless in a snowstorm without easy access to food.

Watering is a crucial part of wild horse life, particularly since most horses now live in regions with limited water supplies. The arid or semi-arid landscapes of the West have only a few natural watering sites. Horse herds tend to home on regular watering places whenever possible, a fact that makes them vulnerable to horse hunters who stake out traps at watering holes. Seldom do individual bands wander more than five to ten miles from water.

They prefer to water in a group, approaching the drinking spot cautiously – it is perhaps the wild horse's most routinely hazardous moment – and taking turns at the water in order of social status. The band stays together, approaching, drinking, and leaving as a unit. If two bands use the same water supply, they usually visit in rotation. Wild horses water at least once a day in normal weather and more often when temperatures rise.

In modern-day Nevada and other regions where they compete with cattle, wild horses may drink as often from man-made watering tanks or ponds as from natural sources. All that is required is a pool of water deep enough for the horse to immerse its lips and suck up the liquid. A wild horse may paw out a shallow depression to allow a pool to accumulate.

Of course, eating and drinking habits cause the most friction between wild horses and western cattle ranchers. There is little confirmed scientific research on the topic and partisan opinion has much to do with how people view the subject, but there can be little doubt that horses are aggressive users of the range. They are such efficient eaters that they can devastate a specific area if overcrowding forces them to wring the last bit of resource from it.

Whether this is a cause for long-term alarm is still something of a question mark, but cattle ranchers are easily (and understandably) convinced that wild horses deprive cattle of grass and water. In the mountain and semi-desert regions of the West, where most wild horses are now concentrated, cattle raising is a marginal enterprise at best, so even slight threats raise the anxieties and antagonism of ranchers. Wild horse herds that clip the grass and shoo cattle from water tanks seem like monsters.

When left undisturbed in areas of sufficient food and water, wild horses breed rapidly, a further cause for ranch-house anxiety.

Just how fast horses increase their population is still a matter of controversy. Only within the last 15 years have the western herds been relatively unmolested by mustangers, and no one is quite certain how many horses there were at any given point (it is notoriously difficult to count wild horse herds accurately, even from the air). Yet, it seems clear that wild horse herds thrive when left alone in a habitat that has what naturalists call sufficient "carrying capacity" – enough food and water to sustain a growing population.

Mares reach breeding age in the wild by their third year. As part of a harem band, they can be expected to produce foals on a regular basis so long as they are attended by a stallion during the crucial periods of estrus (sexual interest) and ovulation, which occur in cycles during specific parts of the year. The horse's gestation period is roughly 340 days, so an active and healthy mare can produce foals at a relatively high rate. The rate of successful conception among wild horses appears to be nearly double that of domestic horses.

When a pregnant mare is ready to deliver, she moves away from the band to be by herself. The actual birth is swift – barring complications – and may take no more than 10 or 15 minutes. Nature has designed horses, like most plains-grazing animals, to spend as short a while as possible in the birth process so as to minimize the vulnerability to predators. Once the foal is expelled, the mare vigorously licks the newborn, both cleaning the baby and providing stimulating tactile sensations.

Foals spend little time adjusting to the world. Within a matter of a few moments, a newly born horse attempts to stand. In a remarkably short period – usually less than an hour – the foal is on its feet and able to move along with its mother, ready to rejoin the family band while nursing and still closely attached to the mare. A birth causes only a slight discontinuity of the band's activities.

Ties between mother and child are close for the first few days and weeks, but the bond is not irreparable. If a foal and its mother are separated during a scramble, for example, the mare generally shows little inclination to search out and protect the foal once the newborn is able to run with the band. Under less stressful circumstances, a foal generally stays close to its mother during the first five or six months of its life, gradually becoming more certain and independent as its grows. Stallions, on the whole, don't pay much attention to foals.

Physical characteristics that impress humans as mildly interesting or even annoying when observed in domestic animals are seen in proper context among wild horses. The animal's acute, specialized vision, for example, is a highly developed defense in the wild horse, although it creates a considerable problem for racing trainers and is the root of the invention of blinders.

Wild horses are range animals with a pressing need to detect and identify danger at long distance, allowing time to flee. Thus, the eye of the horse takes in an extremely wide area, panoramic in scope, that is simultaneously general – giving a large overall picture from horizon to horizon – and tightly focused immediately in front of the horse. Relative to body size, the horse has one of the largest eyes of all mammals, and the placement of the eyes on the head, coupled with the extreme wide angle of vision, means a horse can scan forward, sideways, and behind with only a slight turn of the head.

This results in a view of the world hard for humans to imagine: the horse sees a full image of nearly everything all around it but can't sharply concentrate on anything outside a narrow band. This sort of vision is perfectly suited, however, for spotting danger a long way off.

The horse's hearing is also acute. They may not be able to detect frequencies of sound much beyond the range of human hearing, but horses can turn their ears to home in on specific sounds, and they appear to be extremely sensitive to vibrations picked up from the ground through the bones of the feet and legs.

Smell and taste in horses are closely inter-related, with a bundle of fine nerve connections between nostrils, nose, muzzle, and mouth. All the senses are linked in a system designed to set off the horse's primary defense: flight.

Unquestionably, the greatest glory of horseflesh is to run – in the words of the Koran, "to fly without wings."

Physically, the horse is a well-developed mechanism for sustained running. The animal's relatively compact body has masses of powerful muscle bunched at the upper legs, providing the most power for the least expenditure of energy. The long legs have great extension and leverage – to the point of running always on the toenails, which is what hooves really are – forming an effective pulley system of bone and tendon. The heart and lungs are large compared to total body size and give the horse a very high aerobic capacity for sustained exertion. And the horse's large brain and finely tuned nervous system allow coordination of all these physical attributes.

Horses in the wild can simply outrun all predators, save those equipped with planes or helicopters.

When a member of a wild horse band, usually the guardian stallion, perceives a threat, the response is headlong, almost panic flight. Instinct urges escape. Large herds may stampede heedless of good sense and scatter over a large area. Family bands, on the other hand, tend to be more controlled and seek escape routes as a group, following the lead of the senior mare. The flight response is powerful, however, and most wild horses cease to flee only when hounded to the point of total exhaustion.

When running his band from danger, or indeed during more peaceful moments, the stallion uses a wide variety of verbal and physical signals to communicate. For example, a wild stallion may use a sharp, loud whistle through the nostrils, a sound rarely heard among domestic horses, to alert his band. More common is the familiar neighing sound, usually employed in times of milder distress. The nicker, a soft, breathy sound, is heard most when horses are in repose and content. Mustangers approaching a band or herd of wild horses tried to judge the mood of the animals from the quality of the sounds.

Although they can be spooked by lightning (western thunderstorms are sometimes terrifying spectacles) or other unusual phenomena, wild horses have few occasions to flee non-human adversaries. In earlier days, cougars were a menace and often killed horses for food – old-time westerners believe that the big cats, once tasting it, preferred horsemeat above all other game – but the cougar has almost disappeared today. Horses were particularly susceptible to attacks by mountain lions springing from trees or rocks onto the prey's back. The horse's vision provides warning against threats from ground level, but a horse has a difficult time seeing anything above.

Bears were also once a serious wild horse predator, at least in California, but since there are scarcely any bears left in the Bear Flag State or anywhere else near wild horse habitats, mustangs no longer need fear bears.

Wolves are also few on wild horse ranges, and they apparently prefer the task of killing easier prey than horses, whose speed and endurance make them difficult to catch and whose strength and size make them difficult to kill. Of course, sick, young, debilitated, or solitary horses may become targets.

Nature equipped *Equus caballus* well for unfettered life in the right environment. Only the meddling and incursions of the human animal have damaged the horse's ability to thrive in the wild.

Wild horses and cows don't mix.

From the end of the Civil War to the mid-20th century this iron fact determined the decline of the wild horse from unimaginable numbers roaming the plains to a fragment hiding in nasty places most domestic animals cared not to go. When Americans began to fill up the empty spaces on the western map with cattle-grazing ranches, the easy days of the wild horse were over.

The greatest reduction in the wild horse herds took place rather quietly, out of sight, during the last decades of the 1800s. Farming and cattle ranching on the Great Plains from Texas to Wyoming meant competition for grasslands, water, and space. The buffalo were exterminated, in part to make way for cattle, sheep, and wheat. Wild horses were more adaptable than the bison, so they never disappeared, but competition for food and rangeland cut their numbers between half and two thirds. Drastic weather, such as recurring drought or the catastrophic blizzard winter of 1886-87 killed tens of thousands of horses (and cattle as well).

Moreover, as ranchers moved into horse territory, they tried to rid themselves of the pesky herds by shooting as many stallions as they could, thus cutting off the breeding cycle. Politically powerful livestock associations in most of the western states secured passage of favorable maverick or estray laws that allowed them to claim ownership of wild horses and thus gave license for hunting them down.

There were pockets in the West, however, where horses were tolerated. Nevada, on the whole one of the least promising places for agriculture, became the center of the wild horse population. Horses survived in other scattered enclaves in Wyoming, Montana, Colorado, Oregon, Utah, Idaho, and Oregon. Anywhere ranching was thin was potentially a place for wild horses, even though it meant a change from range roaming to life in foothills, stone canyons, and dry desert edges.

In central and northern Nevada, for example, the terrain is a series of mountain chains with innumerable hidden canyons and valleys whose entrances are barred by juniper and pinon. Horses found it possible to retreat into these hidden spots and thus avoid death or capture.

In regions where the horse herds were not a direct, overwhelming threat to ranchers there developed a reasonably easy-going relationship. Ranchers tolerated the herds, and in fact at various times regarded them as an additional economic resource. There were cycles of demand for horses: as cow ponies, as power to pull plows in the farmlands of the South and Midwest, and then as cannon fodder during the Boer War, the Spanish American War, and World War I.

Moreover, capturing wild horses provided unequalled sport. As Dobie wrote: "To rope and ride a 'desert horse' was an achievement beyond the pale of commonplace living. Like the bear rug in a city doctor's office, a mustang under saddle bore testimony to prowess out in the beyond."

Mustanging – whether for fun or profit – was not easy. Wild horses were not only fleet but intelligent and, once eluding capture, then tended to become increasingly difficult to find and collect. At the turn of the century, mustangers risked life, limb, and saddle ponies when they attempted to ride down mustangs. The wild horses often ran domestic stock flat into the ground, and many a mustanger ended up afoot after a lung-bursting chase that left his mount dead or lame. It was a difficult way to make a few dollars.

Professional mustangers learned the tricks of the trade and developed techniques that at least gave them an even chance of rounding up something for their trouble. Amateurs, usually from the East and attracted by the romance of horse hunting, discovered whatever they knew of polite horses had little relevance to mustangs. Wild horses were cautious and clever and didn't behave like Old Dobbin.

The most obvious (and primitive) approach was to run mustangs to exhaustion through relay teams. This was a time-consuming technique that never guaranteed success. A team of riders might chase a band for days and still never get close enough to uncoil their lariats, or the capture might fail at the end because roping even a tired wild horse was not simple.

Canny mustangers captured individual wild horses with buried box traps that caught mustangs by the foot with a dragline device and slowed them for roping. Others turned Judas horses in with wild bands, hoping to influence the mustangs toward gentleness – a trick that worked indifferently. One of the best methods was to concentrate on the weak point in horse behavior: mustang bands needed water daily. Mustangers staked out selected watering holes and "spooked" the alternatives as a way to force horses into corral traps. Thirst eventually overcame caution, and when the horses finally came to drink, the traps were sprung by concealed mustangers; however, waiting patiently in a hidden blind all day and all night was not something most cowpokes relished.

The most-used technique was to build a disguised corral in a band's home range and then try to run the horses into it before they realized what happened. While a careful and experienced mustanger might capture several horses at once this way, it was not easy. Material for building corrals in remote places was scarce, the labor was considerable, and the slightest mistake in site or camouflage spooked the mustangs and left the mustanger with nothing but sweat and frustration to show for his effort.

The greatest mustang hunter, Charles "Pete" Barnum, who came to Nevada in 1904 and personally supervised the capture of thousands and thousands of wild horses over the following 20 years, invented a collapsible canvas corral that was lightweight, portable, and quick to assemble. Coupled with his keen understanding of mustang behavior, Barnum's corral put horse capture on a reasonably commercial basis.

The object of these old-time mustangers was to capture live horses for sale. But the days of a market for horsepower were short. As more and more gasoline-powered cars and tractors appeared on America's roads and farms, fewer and fewer horses were needed. After World War I, the game changed drastically, altering mustang-hunting from a low-key semi-sport to an enterprise of cruel and grisly exploitation.

In the early 1920s, chicken feed manufacturers in California began to use wild horses as their raw material. They created a demand for horseflesh not in its living form but as ground-up protein. And the chicken feed manufacturers persuaded the railroads to ship horses at a special "chicken feed rate," which meant the usual standards for caring for livestock in transit need not apply. Mustangs were crammed into freight cars at railheads and shipped to California without food or water, allowed to suffer and die from overcrowding, starvation, and thirst. Mustanging became a brutal business.

Even more catastrophic was a change in social behavior among Americans. As the nation became increasingly urbanized in the 1920s, more and more people came to own pets, who demanded artificial care and feeding. In 1923, the first can of dog food was packed in Rockford, Illinois; by 1933, more than 29 million pounds of canned pet food were being processed yearly – most of it cooked mustang. The result was devastation of the remaining western herds. Tens of thousands of wild horses were rounded up to feed the nation's poodles.

An additional blow was dealt in the mid-1930s when the federal government at last began to take a more active role in managing the western grasslands. Decades of ill-considered overuse of rangelands by cattle ranchers had begun to tell on the quality of the grazing lands. Cattlemen were quick to blame wild horses, but the ranchers' short-sighted practices were probably the real culprits. Whoever or whatever was to blame, the Taylor Grazing Act of 1934 established a new system whereby federally owned rangelands were allotted to ranchers and use was to be regulated. The goal was to avoid depletion of resources by a rest and rotation cycle that allowed over-grazed land to recover.

The wild horses, of course, were seen as uncontrollable elements in what was to be a well-ordered management of range. Cattlemen and the federal agencies charged with overseeing the new regulations regarded the horse as a menace to be removed. Once again open season was declared, and during the following decades, advancing technology put the future of wild horses in dire jeopardy.

Disagreement arose in the 1950s over just what the modern wild horse is and where it came from.

There was little argument that the first wild horses were imported by the Spanish or that for centuries the majority of mustang herds were of an Andulusian breed based on North African Barb stock. In South America, the offspring of these animals survive in great numbers. The *criollo* horses of the southern hemisphere still show remarkable resemblance to the Spanish horses of the 16th and 17th centuries.

The wild horse herds in North America, however, are obviously different – demonstrating, for the most part, considerable variation from the early Spanish breed and major differences between places in the West. Some wild horses are large, attractive animals; others are scrawny and ugly, bordering on genetic defects; only a few appear to be, perhaps, real Spanish-style mustangs.

The question was not trivial. Humans – especially humans interested in horses – have rather intense reactions to the appearance and breeding of horses. Therefore, the worth of wild horses has often been judged on these grounds.

Horse lovers in general seem to find certain physical characteristics more pleasing than others. Size is usually a major factor: the larger and taller a horse (up to a point) the more impressive and worthwhile it seems. If size and "fineness" of features are combined, as they are generally in the thoroughbred, the result is a widely accepted ideal of horseflesh, although some fanciers prize sculpted heads, as in Arabians, ahead of height or weight.

We also react strongly to colors in horses. The definite, smooth shades of solid color that characterize most domestic breeds – a result in most cases of selective breed manipulation by humans – is the most generally attractive, although slightly roaned grays (white hairs mixed evenly with darker color) are also pleasing, especially if the animals are attractively groomed. Horses with color patterns may be acceptable, but only if the patterns are regular and cleanly defined.

Few traditional North American wild horses fit this description. Most were small, seldom weighing more than 700 or 800 pounds and standing only 12 to 14 hands (about four to four and a half feet) at the shoulder. Their heads were sometimes large, with a "Roman nose" convex bulge, and they came in many colors and patterns, some almost riotous.

This divergence from common prejudices and preferences led many to devalue the mustang, regardless of its true attributes.

In fact, size has little to do with quality. The original Spanish horses were short-legged, and – like most North African breeds – they had one less vertebra than their cousins bred in the colder lands of the north, so Spanish stock was stubby from nose to tail. This compactness gave wild horses agility and was probably related to the mustang's fabled endurance.

The folklore of mustanging recounts story after story about how grass-eating wild stallions could run bigger, grain-fed American horses into the ground. The U.S. Army discovered to its dismay that the scruffy, tiny Indian cayuse was almost guaranteed to leave cavalry mounts gasping and exhausted. And, when the U.S. Bureau of Animal Industry sponsored a 2,400-mile overland endurance race in 1897, two western brothers won easily on 700-pound mustangs fresh off the range.

Moreover, color in horses is entirely unrelated to other characteristics, even though many human observers have lost sight of this fact. Multi-colored horses are not the result of hybridization or the mating of light animals with dark, but rather mixed color is an inherited trait, passed to offspring through specific genes. We associate solid color phases with the "better" breeds only because patterned horses have been ruthlessly excluded from breeding registries, thus eventually eliminating the color genes that produce multi-colored patterns. There are no spotted thoroughbreds because no horses with spotted pattern genes are allowed to be officially registered as thoroughbreds.

Ironically, this practice excluded one of the most gorgeous animals ever to stand on four legs: the first son of the champion thoroughbred racer Secretariat. The foal came from a test mating between the chestnut stallion and an Appaloosa mare, herself ultimately the result of selected breeding of wild horses by the Nez Perce Indians of Idaho. Even though the offspring of this union had his father's sleek, reddish color and the characteristic white rump "blanket" of his mother's line, in addition to superb conformation, neither the thoroughbred nor the Appaloosa registries allowed the animal a place in the official record.

Interbreeding has probably influenced wild horse herds for a long time. As soon as the first Northern European-bred horse strayed from its master and joined a wild herd, new genes were introduced into the West, and the purity of the Spanish line began to change.

Moreover, in the late 19th and early 20th centuries, stockmen purposely introduced new strains into wild horse populations. Early ranchers in Nevada, for example, regarded the open-range wild horse herds as a source of income, and they discovered the market was better for larger, sleeker horses than for the small mustang. The ranchers turned loose thoroughbred or thoroughbred-related stallions to mate with the mustang mares, and later captured and sold the offspring. In some places, very large, cold-blooded breeds such as Percheron, Clydesdale, or Norman stallions served to "breed up" nearby wild horse bands.

While the results of such practices were worth more in the marketplace, especially when selling to the British during the Boer War or the French during World War I, there is little to demonstrate the crossbreeds were superior to the originals. In fact when ranchers tried to use crosses between draft horses and mustangs as cowponies, they usually discovered the breeding experiments had produced what cowpokes called a "Percheron Puddingfoot" – a horse larger than the average mustang cowpony but without the desired native agility.

By the same token, bred-up horses usually lacked the great reserves of mustang endurance. As Will James, who worked in the West as a cowboy, wrote in 1923: "If I had my pick between a $1,000 Arabian steed and a common fuzztail, I'd much rather select the one with the snort and buck, because I know the trail between suns is never too long for him, no matter how scarce the feed and water may be."

In some cases, the mixing was unintentional. During the Great Depression of the 1930s, for example, thousands of Great Plains farmers went broke and abandoned their livestock, some of which probably joined the wild herds.

When all of these breed influences were added to the meagre fare of wild horses driven into marginal areas, the results were often horses that looked terrible. Wild horses were stunted by lean years, and strange breeding sometimes produced ungainly, even grotesque conformation in some herds. Coats grew shaggy, manes and tails grew long, and the general appearance of many wild horses tended toward the disreputable.

Western ranchers who wanted wild horses off the cattle ranges used the worst-looking examples as excuses to call for the extermination of all herds. They claimed that there was no longer any discernible link between the feral herds and the romantic past of the true Spanish mustang. Why spare such genetic misfits from the pet-food cauldron when they were destroying commercial rangelands?

Other westerners became concerned with re-establishing the type of horse they thought of as the original Spanish mustang. A handful searched western herds for animals that showed the characteristics of the small, traditional horses, and they even established mustang registries as a way to preserve and rebuild mustang lines. In general, they looked for small horses with compact bodies. They also favored dun or grulla-colored horses with the black dorsal stripe and zebra-like leg markings that seemed to indicate ancient lineage.

Advocates on either side are generally unswayed by logic or history, but the facts point to the conclusion that America's wild horses had become by the mid-20th century a mixture of breeds and types. In some places, small, hardy horses still showed evidence of Spanish ancestry, in others the herds were clearly made up of newer strains. In the end, it hardly matters, except to purists or propagandists.

One small, odd-looking, strong-willed woman saved America's wild horses.

In 1950, Velma Johnston was driving down a Nevada highway near her Reno home when she came up behind a stock truck and noticed blood leaking out of the rear of the vehicle. Her curiosity aroused, she followed the truck to its destination, a transportation shipping yard. What she saw when the truck was unloaded sickened her. It also set off a campaign that changed the status of the wild horse from an endangered remnant of the frontier to a protected symbol of the American pioneer spirit.

Johnston had discovered a truckload of recently captured mustangs, bound for the pet-food factory. They were in terrible condition – some grievously injured during capture, all exhausted and suffering. When her protests about the treatment of the horses were ignored, she returned home determined to find out more about who owned the wild horses, who controlled their fates, and what she could do to bring about a change.

By the time Johnston noticed the straits of wild horses, they were on the verge of extinction once again. The market for pet food and the demands of ranchers that wild horses be removed from grazing lands had resulted in a stepped up campaign after World War II to rid the West of mustangs. And the new horse hunters no longer had to rely on pre-industrial methods. Using trucks to reach the remote herds allowed modern mustangers to haul captured animals cheaply and rapidly to shipping points.

The most drastic change, however, was the use of airplanes. Pilots could spot herds much more readily from the air than could mounted hunters, and the tireless airplane ran horses to exhaustion with an efficiency that Pete Barnum could never have imagined. The planes were equipped with sirens to spook the horses, who naturally feared airborne dangers anyway, and the mustangers often loosed shotgun blasts from the planes in order to direct the stampeding animals toward hidden traps.

When pitted against this mechanized onslaught, the remaining wild horses stood little chance of ultimate escape or survival.

Mrs. Johnston, who was the daughter of a rancher,

discovered that such wild horse harvesting was conducted by commercial mustangers who operated under license from the federal Bureau of Land Management, the agency responsible for overseeing use of the rangelands. Removing wild horses to protect the grazing was still the official policy of the government, even though the remaining horses were few in number and seldom ventured onto lands where they competed with cattle. As in many other western states, vast tracts of land in Nevada are still owned by the federal government and ranchers use the range under lease and allotment arrangements. Further investigation only confirmed Johnston's revulsion and anger. She was an unlikely-seeming candidate for a crusade, however. Weighing under 100 pounds, she had been afflicted with polio as a teenager and the treatment left her body twisted and in frequent pain. She wasn't rich, she wasn't powerful, but she was determined.

Dubbed "Wild Horse Annie" by one of her detractors, Johnston reveled in what was intended as a derisive nickname and used it proudly thereafter.

Gathering facts and evidence, she began a crusade to bar airborne hunting of wild horses in her local county. Soon she was campaigning for a state law against the practice. Within a few years, she took her cause to Washington, D.C. Along the way she learned how to get her story into the newspapers, and most importantly, how to organize grassroots support for the beleaguered mustang.

Her masterstroke was to enlist the support of children all over the land. Through letter-writing and publicity, Wild Horse Annie persuaded schoolteachers to have their classes write letters to their Congressmen, urging support for a bill to prohibit horse roundups by air on federal lands. When lawmakers began to receive hundreds of letters from little children, imploring them to save the horses, even the economic influence of the ranch interests couldn't stand in the way.

In 1959, Congress passed what was known as the Wild Horse Annie Bill. It outlawed the use of airplanes to hunt down wild horses and was the first major step in protecting the remaining western herds.

No one was certain, but estimates at the time counted as few as 15,000 to 20,000 remaining wild horses in all of the West, the majority located in the mountains of Nevada.

The new law, however, only solved part of the problem. Commercial horse harvesting was still legal, and mustangers could still use planes to chase horses on private or state-owned lands. Moreover, there was little in the way of enforcement of the law. The BLM was not completely united behind the new statute, and inspectors were few. The destruction of the wild horse had been slowed, but the process continued toward a feared conclusion.

Wild Horse Annie persisted, however, aided by a popular biography for children which spread her crusade even wider. In the mid-1960s, the campaign for an comprehensive law to save the horses received a giant boost when the issue came to the attention of a young television producer named Hope Ryden. Armed with the power of the TV camera and access to air time, Ryden soon became a single-minded publicity machine on behalf of wild horses. Poking into obscure western regions, she photographed horses, collected histories and interviews, and recorded the abuses of the mustangers and bureaucrats. Her book, *America's Last Wild Horses*, along with prime-time news features, did much to keep the issue in the public eye.

Again cranking up the letter-writing machinery and adding the weight of organized eastern humane societies and animal-lovers, the wild-horse defenders brought increasing pressure to bear on Congress and the Department of the Interior during the late 1960s.

Articles appeared in national magazines such as *Time* and *National Geographic*. Wild Horse Annie and her supporers, now organized as the International Society for the Protection of Mustangs and Burros, presented fresh evidence of illegal mustanging, continued abuses, and inhumane practices.

A bill to protect wild horses was introduced in the Senate in January 1970 by Clifford Hansen of Wyoming. Within a few months it drew support from several western political heavyweights in Congress, and lawmakers flooded the legislative hopper with more than 50 save-the-horses bills.

In 1971, the Hansen bill, known as the Wild Free-Roaming Horse and Burro Act, was passed without dissent by both Houses of Congress and signed into law by President Richard Nixon.

The intent clause of the act declared that: "Wild and free-roaming horses and burros are living symbols of the historic and pioneer spirit of the West; that they contribute to the diversity of life forms within the Nation and enrich the lives of the American people; and that the horses and burros are fast disappearing from the American scene. It is the policy of Congress that the wild free-roaming horses and burros shall be protected from capture, branding, harassment, or death; and to accomplish this they are to be considered, in the area where presently found, as an integral part of the natural system of the public land."

The new law forbade not only the killing or capture of horses in the wild, but also made it illegal to sell wild horses for any commercial purpose, curtailing the incentive to round up and slaughter mustangs.

It was also important that the act recognized wild horses as a desirable species on public lands. This had been a major point of contention between save-the-horse advocates and the federal government. Because horses were not a native wild species, but rather descendents of escaped feral animals, they had been denied protection in national parks and forests. It particularly rankled horse lovers that the government protected a great array of game animals, but allowed anyone to shoot horses on sight. Some partisans had even tried to make the argument that horses had never really disappeared in prehistoric times from the North American continent, and were thus eligible for endangered species status.

In general, the Wild Horse Act was all that Annie had worked for. It did, however, present a host of thorny problems to the Bureau of Land Management, the government body designated to enforce the law and charged to find a workable plan of management for the existing wild horse population. Both tasks have proven in the years since to be formidable challenges.

The first difficulty was ignorance. No one except the horse advocates or local ranchers had paid much attention to the wild horses. Data on their numbers, location, habits, and needs were scarce. The BLM gathered as much information as it could and set in motion studies to learn more. Wild horse preserves were established in several states, and the Bureau made every effort, given inadequate funding, to come up with management plans that would protect both the horses and the natural resources of the places they inhabited. At the same time, the BLM was required to pay heed to meeting the needs of cattle ranchers who had grazing rights on land under BLM control.

None of this was simple in 1971, and it has not gotten less complex since.

Within a few years it was clear that the principal goal of the wild horse advocates had been met – the wild horse population ceased to decline and, in fact, began to increase at a healthy pace. Even conservative estimates put the current rate of growth at around 15 percent a year. While this is a testimony to the vigor of the wild horse population in general it has presented major difficulties to the BLM. During the first years of the Wild Horse Act, the Bureau was not allowed to use aircraft in rounding up surplus animals, so the old, less effective methods were tried. As expected, they failed to remove enough horses. In some key regions, particularly Nevada, wild horse herds began to proliferate beyond all expectations.

Even when the BLM wranglers were successful in capturing wild horses, there remained a problem of what to do with them. They couldn't be sold commercially and holding them indefinitely in staging areas was an expensive impracticality. Under the law, the Bureau could have shot horses held longer than 45 days in government corrals, but the BLM has wisely never put its political head on the chopping block by trying such a tactic.

The Bureau sought a solution through the Adopt-A-Horse program. Excess animals that had been removed from the open range were put up for public adoption for a small fee. Anyone who was of legal age, had never been convicted for inhumane treatment of animals, and could demonstrate they had adequate facilities could adopt a wild mustang. Distribution centers were set up in the West (more have been added since in the Midwest and Southeast), and prospective adopters needed only to show up. fill out the papers, pay the fee, and take home a genuine wild horse.

The arrangement worked well in some cases. Young horses and those in good health were suitable candidates for domestication, if the new owners were knowledgeable and patient. But the animals were, indeed, wild and required a slow transition from free-roaming range horses to gentle riding stock. Just the change in diet from grass and rough browse to hay or grain called for careful attention. And many wild horses were in less than sleek condition when captured, often carrying diseases or parasites. New owners had to be prepared for veterinary bills as part of the price of owning a bit of the Old West.

In addition, only younger horses made good pets. Horses that had roamed free until the age of seven or eight seldom adapted to life in the backyard corral. They resisted human attention and often failed to measure up to the expectations of the people who went to considerable effort to adopt them.

New problems were added to the Adopt-A-Horse program in 1982, when the Reagan Administration's pay-as-you-go policies mandated a steep increase in the adoption fee. The price jumped from $25 to $200. When added to maintenance and veterinary costs, this pushed owning a mustang into the realm of luxury for many people, and adoptions declined. The fee has since been reduced to $125, but is still higher than wild horse advocates desire. There are strong signs currently that the adoption market is saturated.

The BLM is now allowed to round up horses by helicopter, which reduces the problem of overcrowding on limited range in some areas of the West. However, in parts of Nevada the horse herds are keeping more than one jump ahead. They have overrun parts of a reserve set up at Nellis Air Force Base, for example, and encroach daily on homeowners who built houses in outlying developments. Housewives who like to watch horses scampering in the distance at sundown find it nonetheless disconcerting to have stallions browsing the backyard.

It is nearly impossible to find impartial observers when it comes to the wild horse "controversy." The topic inflames passions, and discussions usually generate more heat than light. The followers of Wild Horse Annie (she died in 1977) are still active, vigilant, and ready to swing a political baseball bat against the head of the first federal bureaucrat who threatens to damage the status of wild horses. They have fought off several recent attempts to alter the prohibitions on selling horses commercially or to change the grazing laws. At the same time, western ranchers see generations of work and tradition threatened by encroaching herds, and they protest vigorously that the horse population is raging out of control and destroying the economic basis of ranching on lands for which they have paid good money to graze cattle.

Ironically, the ranchers who were initially favorable toward the protection of wild horses are now those suffering most. Shortly after the Wild Horse Act was passed, the BLM offered ranchers the chance to claim wild horses and have them removed for sale. Many ranchers, especially in the more remote valleys of Nevada, passed up the opportunity, at least in part because they regarded scattered horse bands as part of the atmosphere of ranching. Fifteen years later, the same ranchers are faced with a devastating problem. The herds have increased tenfold and taken over most of the water, even the facilities maintained at great expense by the ranchers, and destroyed most of the good graze. This land is in a delicate balance, and the terms of the ranchers' grazing rights agreements with the BLM require resting sections in turn. The horses pay no attention, so the ranchers find themselves in violation of their agreements and in jeopardy of losing grazing rights because of horses they are not able persuade the BLM to control.

Western environmentalists can be found on both sides. Some believe the wild horses are causing irreparable damage to mountain and grazing ranges. Others see the animals as part of a desirable balance of life.

The BLM is caught in the middle, charged with a difficult, perhaps impossible, set of tasks. And the Bureau's problems are unlikely to decrease in the near future. Some fear that in selected regions the horse population is close to the edge of disaster: able to survive in good years, but vulnerable to a repetition of some of the bad winters of the past. Unfortunately, much of the impending crisis is to be seen only in remote areas, far away from the casual eyes of the public.

More prominently displayed are the thousands of head of captured horses for which no homes can be found. Between 1985 and 1987, the BLM rounded up more than 33,000 "surplus" horses at a cost of $50.7 million. Nearly 20,000 – half the number left roaming in the wild – were stuck in government corrals, waiting a disposition that no one in the government clearly foresees.

Despite the current and potential difficulties, there is no doubt that the future of the wild horse in America has been secured against what seemed an inevitable doom only 30 years ago. It is impossible that the vast herds of the past will ever again fill the western plains, but it is also certain that our grandchildren will be able to see a wild horse if they wish.

The image of a wild stallion, outlined by the setting sun against a pure mountain sky, makes us believe, with Shakespeare, that the horse "is pure air and fire, and the dull elements of earth and water never appear in him."

Wild horses of America are colorful, enduring symbols of freedom and the western frontier. They have roamed free in the American West for more than four centuries, and 40,000 to 50,000 wild horses still live in Wyoming, Nevada, Oregon, Colorado, and parts of other western states. America's wild horses now are found mostly in mountainous regions or near the edge of desert lands, but once they ran in vast herds – numbering in the millions – across the Great Plains of the United States. Wild horses conjure for us visions of a free life, galloping amidst breathtaking landscapes and flowing open spaces.

Wild horses are extremely social animals. They prefer to live in relatively small family bands made up of several mares and usually a single dominant stallion. This harem-like arrangement also includes numbers of foals and younger horses still attached to their mothers. The size of the bands varies from region to region in the West and depends, to a large degree, on the quality of the range available for supporting wild horses. Occasionally a band will include more than one stallion, but this is unusual. Wild horses live alone only when forced to, and they will make great efforts to seek companionship. They are almost always seen in groups – feeding, drinking, grooming, and socializing.

Although they may seem similiar to humans, wild horses behave very differently from the domestic animals we see on the farm or at the race track. Once freed from the constraints of human care, horses revert rapidly to their natural habits. They are plains-grazing animals, closely related to the zebras and wild asses of Africa and Asia, and they prefer a free-roaming life amid broad expanses of grasslands. The small family units move about on a 15 to 20-mile home range, traveling together from place to place in search of food and water, which they need each day. As grazers, they have been the objects of predators throughout the ages, so horses in the wild are ever-vigilant for dangers. They use their remarkable eyesight to identify potential threats at long distance, and wild horses are seldom caught unalert.

A dominant stallion, such as this gray roan in Wyoming's Green Mountain region (above and facing page top), keeps a close watch on his harem and offspring. He communicates his wishes through a large selection of sounds and actions, including nips and bites when needed. The two most important duties for a stallion in the wild are to protect his band from outsiders and to breed new horses.

The mustang herds of Wyoming (previous pages, above, facing page and overleaf) are relatively well off compared to herds in other parts of the West. The Wyoming habitat includes good grass range and has gentler topography than the mountains and deserts of Nevada. Wyoming's horses have been well protected and managed, and their handsome appearance reflects a peaceful life.

52

Traditional wild American mustangs, illustrated by these Wyoming horses (above and facing page), have distinctive characteristics. They are short in stature, weigh only between 700 and 900 pounds on average, and show almost all possible color combinations. Mustangs are short-backed and have one fewer vertebra than most other breeds. Their compact conformation contributes to their legendary endurance and toughness – two necessary characteristics for life in the wild. The riot of colors make a herd of mustangs an attractive sight. Color patterns are inherited genetic traits and appear regardless of parents' color. Although it is a matter of minor controversy, these Wyoming mustangs are probably very similar to the original Spanish horses of the 16th century, which were an Andalusian breed, based on North African Barb stock. Sympathetic ranchers in Wyoming in the 1950s began a still-active Spanish Mustang Registry to help preserve the old-style wild horse.

The wild horses of Wyoming's Red Desert (facing page top, right and overleaf) are among the largest and sleekest of America's wild horses. In contrast to the Spanish-type mustangs of the Green Mountain and Pryor Mountain regions, the Red Desert wild horses are taller and heavier, weighing up to 1,200 pounds each. The reasons for the larger size can be traced to the practice by local ranchers of culling small stallions from the wild horse herds and replacing them with large, Northern European cold-blooded stallions of Percheron or Belgian breeding. The results over time were big, powerful horses with little tendency toward mixed color patterns. Wild horses in northern Nevada (above and facing page bottom) were also "bred up" by infusions of outside stock and differ from the classic mustang.

Horses are endowed with unusual vision, which allows them to detect and identify potential threats at long distance. Set high on a long neck and head, the wild horse's large eyes give an extraordinarily wide field of sight, seeing forward, sideways, and backward – all at the same time. The horse takes in a huge panorama in one glance and is particularly acute at noticing movement anywhere in the range of sight.

With only a slight turn of its head, a horse is able to scan a full circle, an amazing and valuable asset for a plains-grazing animal. The disadvantage is the inability to focus sharply on anything outside a very narrow area directly in front of the horse's head, and because of the placement of the eye on the head, horses have a very difficult time seeing anything above them.

Horses in the Red Desert area (these pages) have been targets of illegal mustang hunters in recent years, despite well-publicized federal laws protecting all wild horses from capture, killing, or commercial sale. In 1984, for example, two men pleaded guilty to selling 100 horses captured on the Red Desert to a New Mexico slaughterhouse. They were let off with a fine and probation, outraging wild horse protection advocates. Many Americans agree with the assessment of historian J. Frank Dobie that "halted in animated expectancy or running in abandoned freedom, the mustang was the most beautiful, the most spirited and the most inspiring creature ever to print foot on the grasses of America."

Young horses seldom remain with the family band longer than a few years. The stallion drives his filly offspring out of the band to be picked up by some other stud bunch when they reach foal-bearing age. Females are at least assured of a secure place in wild horse society; young males are less fortunate. When colts reach sexual maturity and begin to pose a threat to the dominant band stallion, then they must go, and such young males are seldom tolerated around any other mature stallion's harem. Until they reach the stage that they can claim a harem of their own by defeating a reigning stud, young bachelors often band together in uneasy adolescent alliances. Two beautifully matched young blacks in the Red Desert of Wyoming (overleaf) show the marks of what was probably practice combat, learning the skills needed to win their own bunch of mares.

Wild horses must drink at least once a day, more often in very hot weather, and since most modern-day wild horses live in the arid or semi-arid regions of the West, watering is a constant challenge. They must find pools of standing water because horses drink by immersing their lips below the surface and sucking up the liquid. In the driest conditions, mustangs will paw out a shallow hole to allow water to collect. Wild horses tend to drink less often than domestic horses and in larger quantities at a single visit to a watering source – up to four liters of water at one time. Visits to water are dangerous moments for wild horse bands because it is then they are most vulnerable to attack or capture, and both natural predators and mustang hunters take advantage of the horse's need to drink.

Seasonal views of wild horse country in the Kingsley Mountain district of northern Nevada (these pages) show the sparse vegetation and rugged grazing conditions typical of much modern-day horse range. By nature, horses are grass eaters. They are equipped with large incisors that allow them to clip off grasses efficiently, and tough, enamel-ridged rear teeth that are used to grind the coarse fodder before swallowing. However, horses also can adapt to browsing on scrub brush, tree bark, and other rough foods. Unlike cattle, horses can digest rough browse, and even thrive on it if they get it in sufficient quantities. Horses are also adept at pawing aside snow to reach wintertime food.

By the last years of the 1800s, more and more wild horse herds found their way into the beautiful but forbidding country in northern Nevada. The rugged topography of this area was a key to the survival of wild horses. The land is basin and range country, with a series of sharp north-south mountain chains broken by canyons and hidden valleys. Harried by commercial mustang hunters and cattle ranchers, the horse herds retreated to this difficult terrain in order to stay out of harm's way. Only the most determined horseback mustanger tried to track down wild horses under these conditions.

89

Perhaps it is their self-sufficiency that explains our fascination with wild horses. They inspire admiration, not only because they are free, but also because they do not depend on humans for their well-being. Nothing could be farther from a manicured, board-fenced, Kentucky horse-breeding farm or a New York City bridle path than wild horses running free on the rangelands of northern Nevada (these pages and overleaf), completely independent of human intervention. It's not hard to imagine them equally at home on the steppes of Asia or the savanna plains of Africa. Moreover, horses in the wild serve no function related to the human world; they exist totally for their own purposes, which revolve around the most basic activities – eating, breeding, and staying away from predators. "They really belong," wrote Will James, "not to man, but to that country of junipers and sage, of deep arroyos, mesas – and freedom."

Horses are designed to run. A wild horse has nearly perfect physical equipment to live in open spaces, where speed afoot provides the best defense against danger. The horse's compact body has strong running muscles bunched for power at the shoulder and hindquarters, with long, extended legs to provide maximum leverage. The horse's heart and lungs are highly efficient in order to supply oxygen to the muscles for quick bursts of speed or during prolonged flight. And a sophisticated nervous system and a large brain tie all the horse's physical attributes together. The result is an animal that can run naturally and swiftly from its earliest days. The two most characteristic glimpses of wild horses are to see them looking inquisitively at potential danger or fleeing from it like the wind.

America's wild horses have been known by many names. The term "mustang" derived from a Spanish term for strays of any kind, originally including sheep and cattle, but it came to mean specifically wild horses, especially the Spanish-type horse of the 18th and 19th centuries, examples of which survive today in Wyoming and parts of Oregon. In Nevada, wild horses such as these north of Winnemucca (these pages and overleaf) were often referred to as "Cimarrons" or simply "marrons." Western ranchers and cowboys called wild horses "fuzztails" or "broomtails" because of their unkempt, unclipped tails. One symptom of locoweed poisoning, a frequent wild horse hazard, was an abnormal growth of mane and tail.

Wild horses have inspired tall tales and countless camp-fire stories throughout the West. In the early days, when a cowpoke pitted his skills on horseback directly against a wild stallion, legends grew up around any especially elusive mustang. The most famous was the Great White Pacing Stallion, who was reported all over the American West, from Texas to California. The White Pacer could effortlessly outdistance pursuers, never even breaking into a full run, but keeping on the more controlled pacing gait, no matter how determined the chasers. Darker legends surrounded a Black Devil, a killer wild horse who led his pursuers into tight corners and then attacked. Whatever the truth of the stories, wild horses continue to inflame human imaginations. As one writer puts it, the wild horse is the "liberator of mind pictures."

By the late 1940s, all-out war was declared on wild horses by cattle ranchers and commercial mustang hunters. Using airplanes to run horses to exhaustion, mustangers removed tens of thousands of wild horses from the range and shipped them under horribly inhumane conditions to pet food factories. Although they had led mounted hunters a merry chase, wild horses stood little chance against mechanized human predators. Saved on the brink of extinction by the Wild Horse Act of 1971, the herds are now protected and have proliferated at a rapid pace during recent years, especially in Nevada, where large numbers of wild horses overrun the range set aside for them. The federal Bureau of Land Management faces difficult problems in controlling horse herds while at the same time protecting them as symbols of the American past.

Today's mustang hunters use helicopters and careful methods to capture wild horses for removal. The veteran duo of Dave Catoor (above, left of picture) and Jim Hicks (above, right of picture) are two of the most experienced at gathering horses for the Bureau of Land Management. Catoor, a native of Colorado, has run horses since his childhood and was instrumental in getting the horse protection laws amended to allow the use of helicopters, a more efficient method and much easier on the horses. Hicks, a Vietnam veteran pilot, has worked with Catoor since 1977.

The fortunes of America's wild horse population have taken a dramatic turn since the late 1960s, when perhaps as few as 17,000 remained. The Wild Horse Act of 1971 stopped the deprivations of the herds, and the ensuing years saw at first a slow revival and then a dramatic growth. The BLM has a dual responsibility regarding the growing numbers of western wild horses: to protect and manage wild horses as a national resource and to administer western rangelands for maximum benefit. As the horse herds increased, especially in rural northern Nevada, the conflicts between these two goals intensified. So long as horse herds were small, cattle ranchers were relatively tolerant of them, and many Nevada ranchers neglected to have horses removed soon after the passage of the protection law. Today, the rapidly growing herds spill into areas that ranchers are obligated to leave ungrazed, sharpening the conflict between ranchers and BLM over what to do about removal.

Government wranglers in Nevada move captured horses toward holding pens (above, right) where they will await disposal. No one is quite certain just what to do with all the horses now coming off the Nevada rangelands.

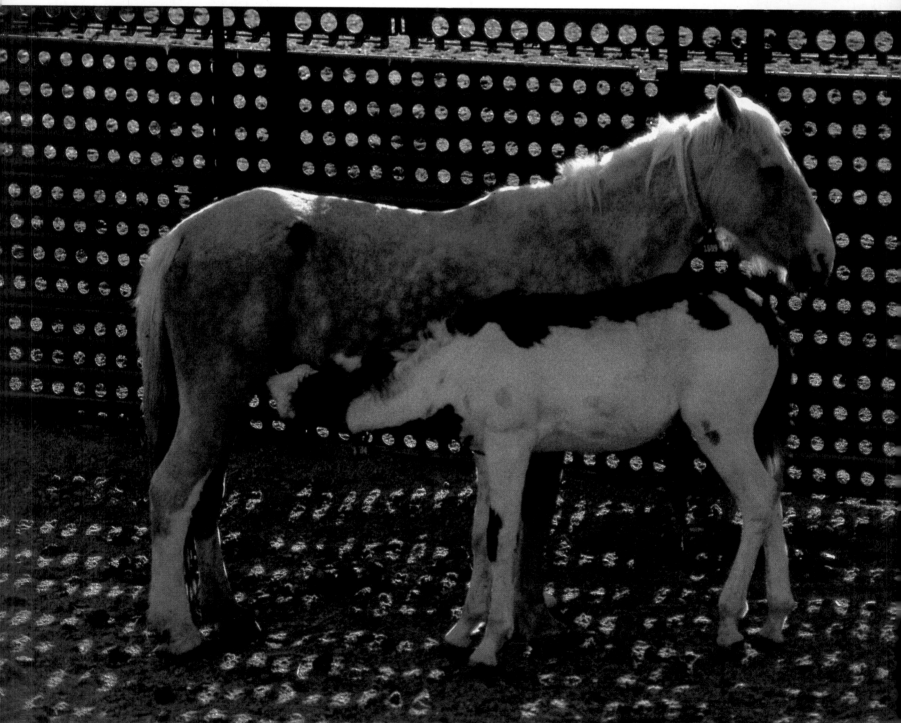

When captured horses began to accumulate in BLM corrals in the late 1970s, the agency devised a plan to offer horses for adoption to the general public for a nominal fee. The Adopt-A-Horse program was a hit, and thousands of formerly-wild horses found new homes all over the nation. The Palomino Valley Wild Horse and Burro Placement Center in Nevada (these pages, overleaf and following pages) is one of several centers run by the BLM. New centers were opened during the 1980s in the midwestern and southeastern U.S., but the program has declined in popularity in recent years in part as the result of increased fees. Only a few of the available horses are now taken for adoption.

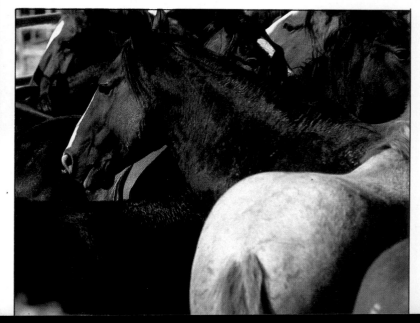

Captivity does not soon quell the
natural competitive instincts of
mustang stallions; they still battle for
dominance, although their days as
leaders of a harem are probably over.
Such spirited horses, accustomed to
freedom and fearful of humans, make
poor adoptees, since they seldom learn
to live quietly as hand-fed pets or riding
horses. The BLM is sensitive about what
happens to excess wild horses, and with
good reasons. Wild horse advocates are
well organized and exert a powerful
grass-roots political force. During
earlier controversies, thousands of
Americans rallied to the call to deluge
Congress with letters on behalf of the
threatened wild horses, and organized
horse lovers stand ready to repeat the
performance if they see the need. Under
the law, the BLM could sell the horses
for slaughter, but such a dangerous
move would doubtless spark a huge new
controversy.

148

149

150

By the late 1980s, the BLM had nearly 20,000 captured horses in its corrals, almost half the total that remained in the wild. Between 1985 and 1987 alone, the agency rounded up 33,000 head, mostly in northern Nevada. The cost to taxpayers to feed the animals was nearly $9.5 million each year. In the face of such numbers, good intent seems a weak device. Solving the problem may come down to finding a way to reconcile the interest of those who want to preserve America's wild horses at all costs as symbols of the American character and frontier spirit and those who want to raise cattle on the sparse western grazing lands. Pro-horse forces point out that any damage to rangelands is more likely caused by cattle than horses. There are 400 head of cattle for each wild horse on BLM-controlled land.